This book
belongs to

- - - - - - - -

Yellow Jersey Press, an imprint of Vintage
20 Vauxhall Bridge Road
London SW1V 2SA

Yellow Jersey Press is part of the Penguin Random House group of companies
whose addresses can be found at global.penguinrandomhouse.com

Penguin
Random House
UK

First published by Yellow Jersey Press in 2016

penguin.co.uk/vintage

A CIP catalogue record for this book is available from the British Library

ISBN 9780224100694

Printed and bound by CPI Moravia Books s.r.o., Pohořelice

Penguin Random House is committed to a sustainable future
for our business, our readers and our planet. This book is made from
Forest Stewardship Council® certified paper.

MIX
Papier aus verantwor-
tungsvollen Quellen
FSC® C083411

COLOURING *the* TOUR *de* FRANCE

JAMES NUNN & WILLIAM FOTHERINGHAM

YELLOW JERSEY

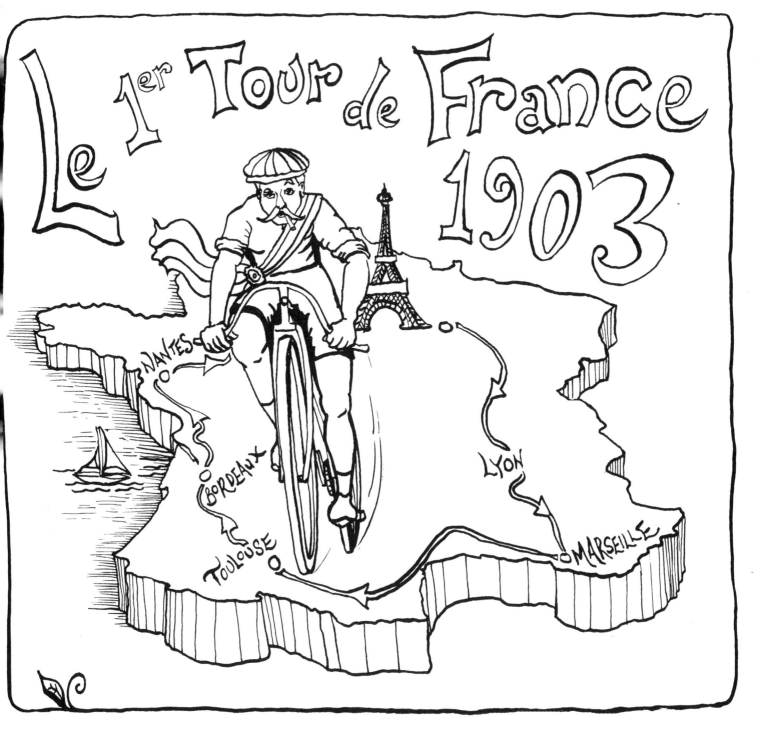

EUGENE CHRISTOPHE
THE ORIGINAL
ETERNAL SECOND 1913

How to cheat № 2: hold the sticky bottle

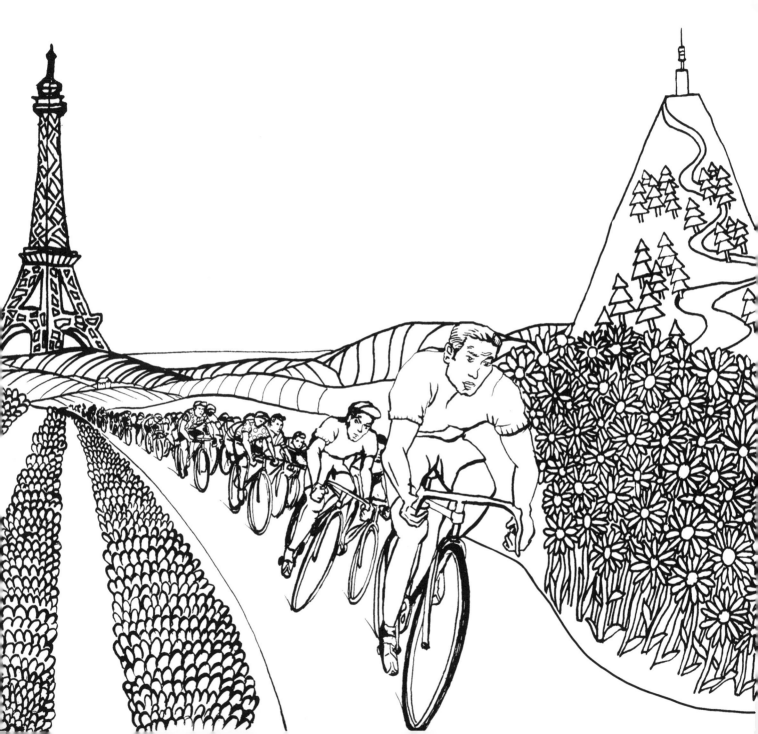

Charles Boty
cycliste de la Résistance

Charly GAUL ~ Angel of the Mountains

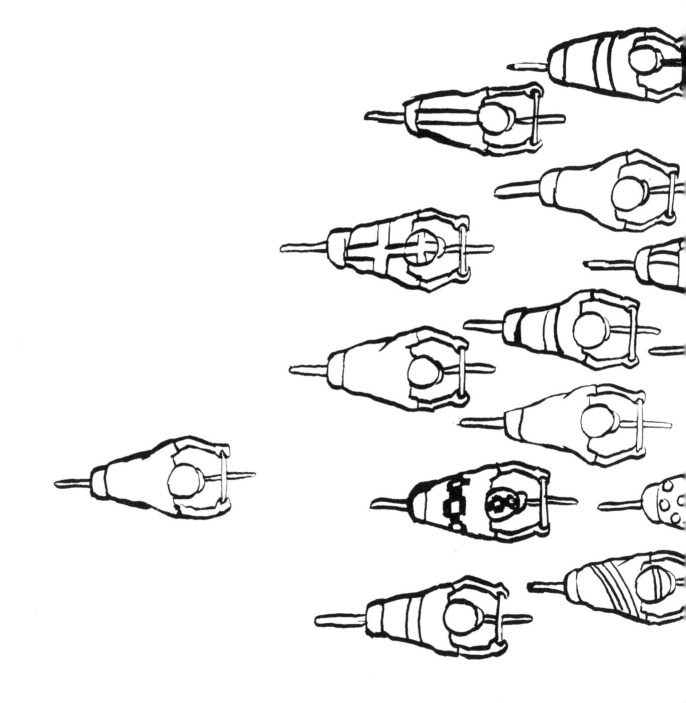

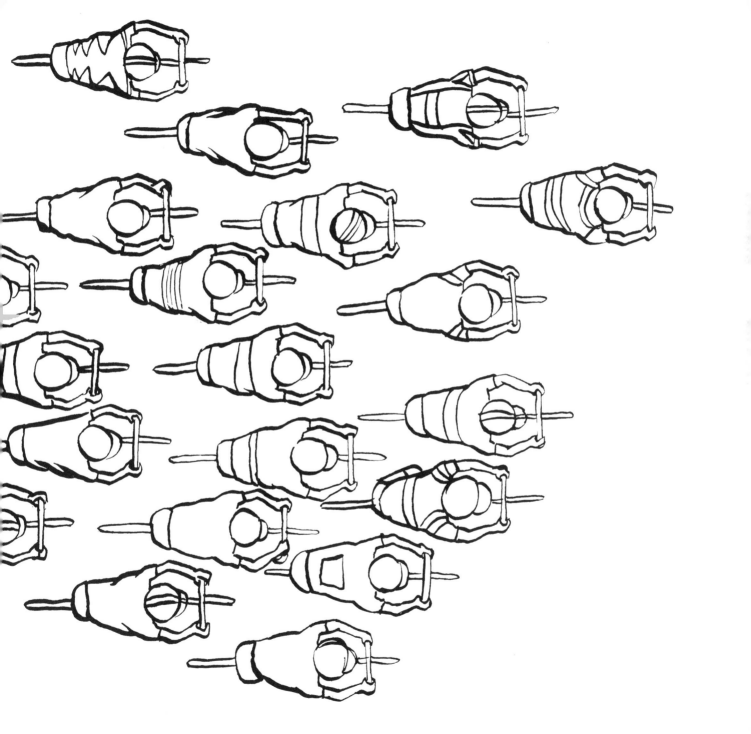

TOM SIMPSON
MONT VENTOUX
1967

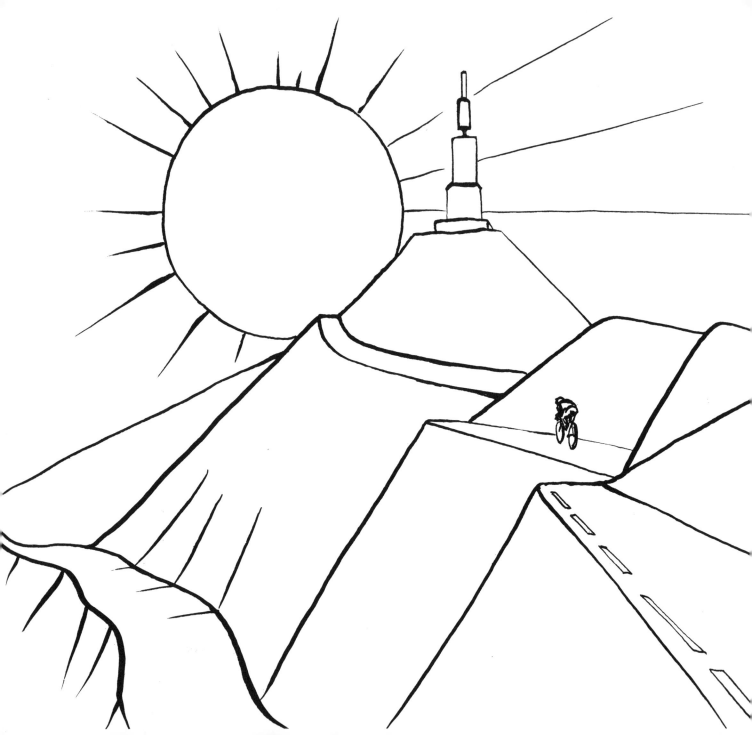

The Cannibal

LUIS OCAÑA
COL DE MENTÉ
1971

A Bestiary of Le Tour

LE PROFESSEUR

LAURENT FIGNON

MIGUEL INDURAIN

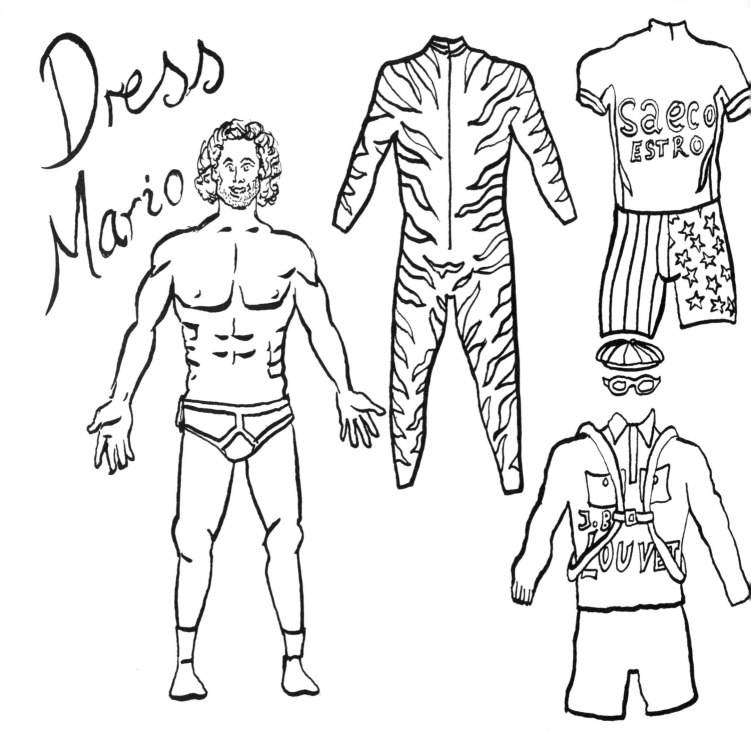

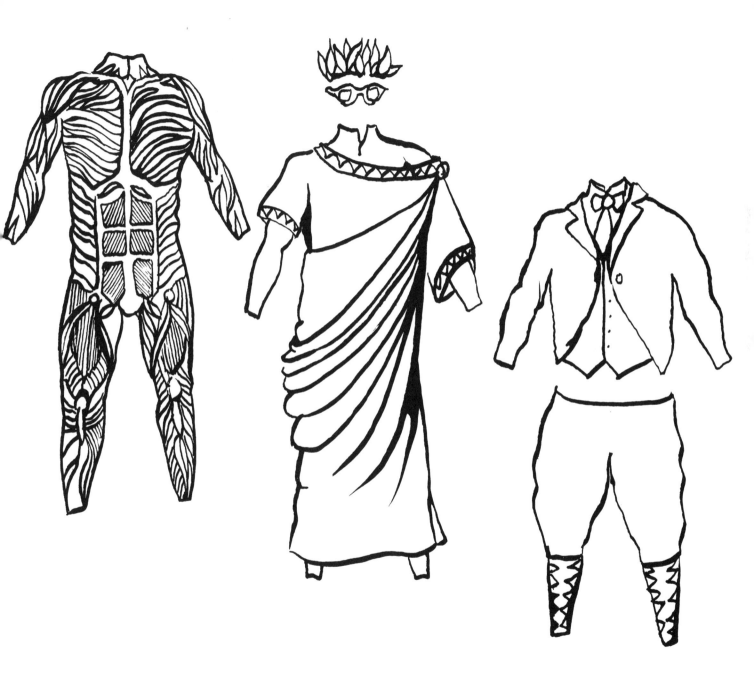

Ceci n'est pas une bicyclette

VENTOUX

...MUST GO UP

CHRIS FROOME, 2016

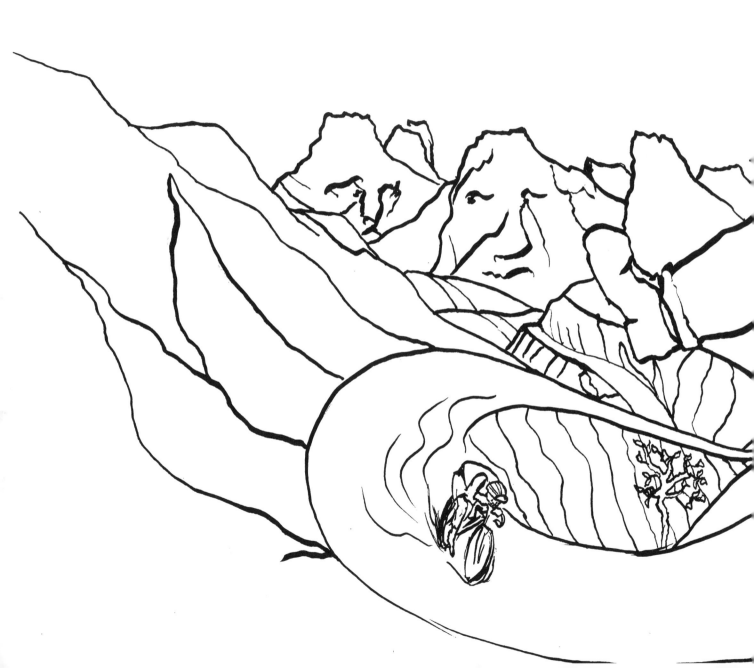

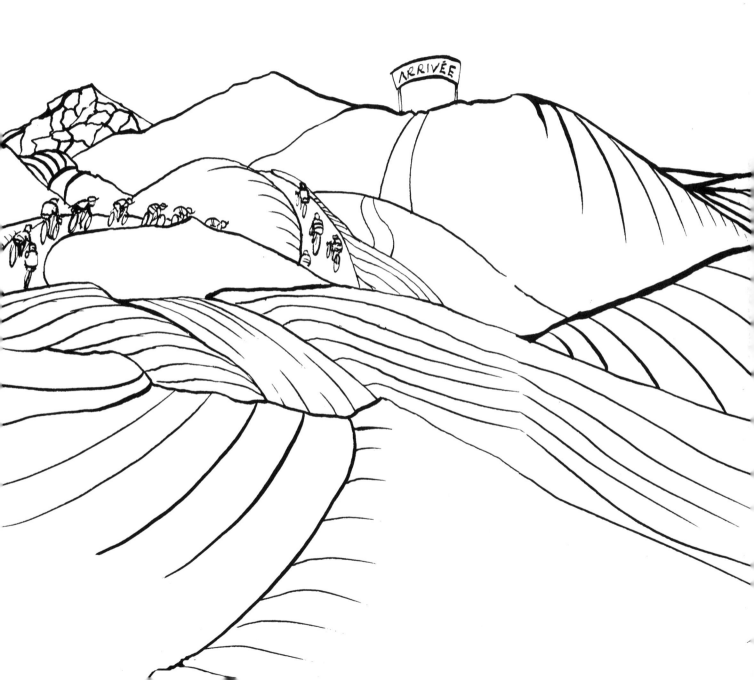

NOTES

HOW TO CHEAT NO 1: TAKE THE TRAIN

After the immense success of the first Tour in 1903, the second saw the first four overall disqualified for various forms of cheating; in the early years there were occasions when riders were alleged to have taken a train instead of riding their bikes.

'ASSASSINS!'

The 1910 Tour was the first to visit the Pyrenees; in appalling conditions as the riders tackled the Col de l'Aubisque, a rider in the lead group – usually held to be eventual winner Octave Lapize – saw a car with their race organisers in it and screamed 'assassins'. Their response was to send future Tours through the Alps.

EUGÈNE CHRISTOPHE, THE ORIGINAL ETERNAL SECOND, 1913

Eugène Christophe repairs his broken fork during the 1913 Tour. He walked over 8km to find a forge and incurred a time penalty for asking a young lad to operate the bellows.

HOW TO CHEAT NO 2: HOLD THE STICKY BOTTLE

The 'Sticky Bottle' is on the borderline between legal assistance and actual cheating, where a rider grabs a bottle from his team car and takes a brief tow to pull himself up to a higher speed. Commissaires are always on the look-out for riders who pull for too long and too often, or who take a straight tow from the car by holding on, usually to the window frame.

CHARLES BERTY

Charles Berty rode three tours between 1935 and 1939, but he is more aptly remembered for his courage as a member of the French resistance. He was responsible for finding safe ground for airdrops of food and ammunition. He was denounced and deported to Mauthausen Concentration Camp where he died on April 18, 1944. In 1948 the Velodrome in Grenoble was named after him.

BARTALI VS. COPPI

Gino Bartali and Fausto Coppi, leading champions and bitter rivals in the golden age of cycling immediately after World War II.

GINO BARTALI, THE PIOUS ONE

Gino Bartali – who won the Tour in 1938 and 1948 – was nicknamed 'the Pious One' and had his own chapel built at his home in Tuscany. He was recognised in 2013 for his efforts to aid Jews during the German occupation of Italy.

PASSING THE BOTTLE

The image of Coppi handing Bartali a bottle – or is it the other way round? – was a key part of the mythology surrounding the pair: just who is helping who and why?

FEDERICO BAHAMONTES, THE EAGLE OF TOLEDO STOPS FOR ICE CREAM

The legendary 'Eagle of the Mountains', Federico Bahamontes, won the Tour in 1959 and took the King of the Mountains title a record six times. After crashing into a cactus as an amateur he hated to descend alone. As well as his legendary mountain attacks, he is famed for once stopping to chat with spectators and eating an ice cream at the summit while waiting for the others to catch up.

CHARLY GAUL, ANGEL OF THE MOUNTAINS

Charly Gaul of Luxembourg was another celebrated mountain climber, winner of the Tour in 1958; 'a murderous climber, turning his legs at a speed which would break your heart,' as a contemporary Raphael Geminiani said. After his retirement Gaul lived as a hermit in a shack in the Ardennes for many years until he rejoined society in 1983. He died in 2005.

LE COL D'IZOARD
Another of the Tour's highest and toughest cols, the Izoard is a visual treat situated to the south of the Alpine town of Briançon. Topping out at 2360m, it includes a section through the Casse Deserte, which resembles Death Valley with its eroded rock pinnacles, and it is associated mainly with names of the 1950s such as three-times winner Louison Bobet and Coppi and Bartali.

JACQUES ANQUETIL AND RAYMOND POULIDOR
France's Jacques Anquetil fought out several Tours de France with his fellow countryman Raymond Poulidor, notably the 1964 race when Anquetil won by just 55 seconds. The pair achieved massive fame in France for their rivalry, but it was the gallant loser Poulidor – who never even wore the yellow jersey in the Tour – who became truly popular.

TOM SIMPSON, MONT VENTOUX, 1967
Legend has it that the final words of the British world champion Tom Simpson before he collapsed and died in 1967 on the fearsome Mont Ventoux were 'put me back on my bike' but the only witness account says, more prosaically, that he was in fact muttering 'on, on, on'.

TOM SIMPSON SHRINE
Tom Simpson's memorial high on Mont Ventoux is now a place of pilgrimage for cycling fans who pedal painfully up the 'Giant of Provence' and leave something – a bottle, a cycling cap – in homage to 'Major Tom.'

THE OBSERVATORY, MONT VENTOUX
The Observatory on Mont Ventoux, a painful goal for amateurs and Tour cyclists alike – with one of the world's greatest views.

THE CANNIBAL
Eddy Merckx is cycling's most successful rider ever: five-times winner of the Tour, also five-times winner of the Giro d'Italia, and winner of 525 races out of the 1800 he rode in his career. Merckx is one of three riders to win all the sport's greatest one-day races. 'The Cannibal' retired in 1978.

L'ALPE D'HUEZ
A ski resort up the Romanche Valley from Grenoble, is the site of one of the Tour's most feared mountain-top finishes.

LUIS OCAÑA, COL DE MENTÉ, 1971
Luis Ocaña's attempt to dislodge Merckx from his supremacy in the Tour came to a bitter end when the Spaniard fell on the Col de Menté in the Pyrenees in 1971.

A BESTIARY OF LE TOUR
Tour riders are often given animal nicknames; on the left-hand page: The Lion (King) – Mario Cipollini; the Penguin – Geraint Thomas; the Rat – Joop Zoetemelk; the Eagle – Federico Bahamontes; the Heron – Fausto Coppi; the Panda – Laurent Jalabert; the Badger – Bernard Hinault; the little Elephant – Marco Pantani; the Flea – Vicente Trueba. On the right-hand page: the Gorilla – Andre Greipel; Le Coq – Joseph Groussard, or the Rooster – Iban Mayo; the Basset Hound – Philippe Thys; the Boar - François Neuville; the Cobra - Riccardo Riccò; the Camel - Tony Rominger; the Bison – Juan Jose Cobo; the Kangaroo – any Australian.

THE BADGER

Bernard Hinault – the Badger – is the last Frenchman to win the Tour de France, back in 1985, and was, like Merckx, one of the four record-holders to win the Tour five times. Like Coppi, Merckx and Anquetil, he achieved the celebrated 'double' of winning the Tour de France and Giro d'Italia in the same year.

L'AMÉRICAIN, LE PROFESSEUR

In 1989, Greg LeMond achieved the closest ever Tour win, by a mere 8 seconds, from the Frenchman Laurent Fignon; and he did so on the final metres of the Tour's closing stage on the Champs-Élysées.

MIGUEL INDURAIN

Miguel Indurain is the only man to have won the Tour five times in a row (1991–95) and as his birthday fell on July 16, Big Mig was usually given a cake in the Tour's start village to mark the occasion.

THE PIRATE

Another distinctive nickname: the Pirate, as the 1998 Tour winner Marco Pantani was known. He was also referred to as Elefantino, or Dumbo, because of his prominent ears.

HOW TO CHEAT NO 3: ASK LANCE

Lance Armstrong remains the Tour's most controversial figure; cancer survivor and seven-time winner, stripped of his titles and given a life ban by the US Anti-Doping Agency after an inquiry that revealed systematic doping in his teams.

DRESS MARIO

Mario Cipollini, the celebrated Italian sprinter, never finished a Tour but turned up at the race in a variety of jerseys and skin suits designed to give his sponsors maximum publicity.

THE TASHKENT TERROR

A legendary crash: the Uzbek sprinter Djamolidine Abdoujaparov goes into the barriers on the Champs-Élysées in 1991.

LE NAUGHTY ÉTAPE

Seven years after the fact, the disgraced Lance Armstrong tells all to Oprah Winfrey in January 2013.

WHERE'S WIGGO?

Sir Bradley Wiggins was the first Briton to win the Tour in 2012; as well as being one of the sport's most versatile champions on road and track, and one of Britain's greatest Olympians; the 'Kid from Kilburn' is also a dedicated Mod and fan of The Who.

'ALLEZ ALLEZ ALLEZ!!!'

The Tour-Devil (TourTeufel) is a German named Didi Senft who dresses up in a red Lucifer suit and runs alongside the riders waving a trident. He's been doing this since 1993 and has become a celebrity in his own right, inspiring a whole generation of fans to put on fancy dress and cheer the Tourmen on.

CHRIS FROOME

Chris Froome's 2016 Tour win, his third, included a stage win at Luchon, where he used this unorthodox position going down a mountain (don't try it at home folks, it's highly dangerous), and an episode on Mont Ventoux where his bike broke. Froome didn't have a spare and took to running in his carbon-fibre-soled shoes.

THE MAN WITH THE HAMMER
'Meeting the Man with the Hammer' is French cycling slang for having a bad day on the bike, or 'hitting the wall' as marathon runners put it.

THE LANTERNE ROUGE
The last rider on the Tour was traditionally given a red lantern to mark his place at the back of the group; the custom died out in the 1960s.

THE BROOM WAGON
These days, most riders climb off at a feed station so they can get straight into a team vehicle but the *voiture balai* still travels along at the very back of the Tour caravan 'sweeping up' riders who have no option but to abandon en route; it is a modern vehicle but still has a *besom* on top as a nod to tradition.

ILLUSTRATOR'S NOTE

The imagery thrown up by this wonderful race is endless. Aside from the riot of colour racing through the sun-drenched countryside, there is an infinite supply of scarcely credible stories; from the endeavours of the early riders to the heroes and villains of the race we know now. Delving into these tales of the Tour and the men whose lives it has consumed one will, at some point, discover Pellos, the pre-eminent illustrator of the Tour from 1932 to 1982. One of the many charms of his drawings is his characterisation of the mountains as malign and mischievous gods and monsters toying with riders for sport. In tribute to him I have occasionally imbued my mountains with a touch of this personality and I urge fans of cycling and illustration alike to seek him out. I hope that this book has a fraction of his panache. It has been so much fun to put these drawings together and I could not have done so without the guidance of William Fotheringham whose knowledge and enthusiasm for the Tour is inexhaustible and whose books have been both a source of inspiration and entertainment. I would also like to thank Rachel Cugnoni, Beth Coates and Nick Skidmore at Yellow Jersey Press for their faith and patience and for the free rein to let the pen go where the wheels took me.

JN, 2016